AN ALBUM OF THE SIXTIES

BY CAROL A. EMMENS

A GROLIER COMPANY

FRANKLIN WATTS
NEW YORK | LONDON | TORONTO | SYDNEY
1981

Cover design by Ginger Giles

Cover photographs courtesy of: United Press International:
upper left and lower right; Wide World Photos: lower left.

Photographs courtesy of: John F. Kennedy Library: opp. page 1, p. 9 (top
and bottom left); United Press International: pp. 4 (top), 13 (bottom), 15
(top), 22 (right), 23, 26 (bottom), 29, 32 (top), 49 (bottom), 53 (top), 58 (bottom), 67, 78, 83 (bottom right), 84; Wide World Photos: pp. 4 (bottom), 5
(top), 30 (top), 32 (bottom); U.S. Army: pp. 5 (bottom), 21 (left); U.S. Navy:
pp. 6 (top), 18 (bottom); German Information Center: p. 6 (bottom); Bob
Jackson: p. 9 (bottom right); Lyndon B. Johnson Library: pp. 10, 13 (top),
14 (top), 26 (top right), 30 (middle and bottom), 53 (bottom right); Consul-
ate General of Israel: p. 15 (bottom); Bob Floper: p. 21 (right); Newark
Public Library: p. 26 (top left); Ronald Haeberle/Time Life Pictures: p. 33;
CBS News: pp. 36, 61; NASA: pp. 39 (left and right), 40, 41 (all), 42 (top);
AT & T Co.: pp. 42 (bottom), 45 (bottom right); Texas Instruments: p. 45
(top left); IBM: p. 45 (top right); General Motors: p. 45 (bottom left); Reynolds Metal Co.: p. 46 (top left); U.S. Fish & Wildlife Service: p. 46 (top right,
bottom right, bottom left); CORE: p. 49 (top); Newark Public Library: pp. 50
(both), 54, 57 (both), 58 (top); Religious News Service: p. 58 (left); David
Redfern: p. 62 (top); Bob Dylan: p. 65 (top left); MGM-TV: p. 70 (top); Bing
Crosby Productions: p. 70 (bottom right); Wisconsin Center for Film & The-
ater Research: p. 71 (top left); Tom & Dick Smothers: p. 71 (top right);
United Artists: p. 75 (top); Martha Swope: p. 75 (bottom left); Columbia
Records: p. 75 (bottom right); L.A. Dodgers: pp. 80, 81 (top); N.Y. Yankees:
p. 81 (bottom left & right); N.Y. Jets: p. 83 (left); Green Bay Packers: p.
83 (top right); NBC: p. 71 (bottom).

Library of Congress Cataloging in Publication Data

Emmens, Carol A
An album of the sixties.

Includes index.
SUMMARY: Text and pictures present
an overview of the political, social, and
cultural events of the 1960's.
1. United States—Civilization—1945–
—Juvenile literature. [1. United States—
Civilization—1945–   ] I. Title.
E169.12.E47   973.92   80–21295
ISBN 0–531–04199–9

CONTENTS

John F. Kennedy

Color by Fabian Bachrach

**THE COLD WAR:
THE LEGACY OF
THE FIFTIES**

During the 1950s, the relationship between the United States and the Communist countries of the world, especially the Soviet Union, was an uneasy one. The threat of war hung over the heads of Americans.

When the USSR launched the world's first satellite, Americans panicked. Rocket expert Wernher von Braun wrote, "Overnight it became popular to question the bulwarks of our society; our public education system, our industrial strength, our international policy, defense strategy and forces, the capability of our science and technology. Even the moral fiber of our people came under searching examination."

As 1960 approached, Americans were unsure of the future. John Fitzgerald Kennedy challenged them to reach new goals.

"ASK NOT WHAT YOUR COUNTRY CAN DO FOR YOU..."

The vote was close, 34,227,096 to 34,108,546, and it swept John F. Kennedy into the White House in 1960. Kennedy's victory over Richard M. Nixon, the Vice-President of the United States, was an upset.

Nixon entered politics in 1946 when he was elected to the House of Representatives. He was elected to the Senate in 1950, but his unethical campaign tactics earned him the nickname "Tricky Dick." Dwight D. Eisenhower, the Republican candidate for the presidency in 1952, selected Nixon as his running mate. They won easily and were reelected in 1956. Nixon was a shoo-in for the Republican presidential nomination in 1960.

His opponent, John F. Kennedy, worked hard to win his party's nomination for the presidency. As a Senator and as a war hero, Kennedy was an ideal candidate except for his age and his religion. He was forty-three, and he was Catholic. No Catholic had ever been elected to the presidency. Kennedy conducted a barnstorming campaign. He easily won primary after primary.

The delegates to the Democratic Convention nominated Kennedy as their candidate on the first ballot. Then he surprised them by choosing his political foe, Lyndon B. Johnson, as his running mate. Kennedy, a Massachusetts Senator, wanted to attract Southern voters, and Johnson was a Texan.

During the campaign, Kennedy blamed the Republicans for Russia's superiority in outer space. He also criticized the military, the schools, and the economy. His major campaign theme was "Mr. Nixon says we've never had it so good. I say we can do better." Kennedy claimed it was time to "move the country forward again."

Nixon's slogan was "Experience Counts." In his speeches he emphasized his accomplishments as Vice-President, and he accused Kennedy of being inexperienced in foreign affairs. Despite rumors that President Eisenhower personally disliked him, the polls showed Nixon in the lead.

Then Nixon made a costly mistake. He accepted Kennedy's challenge to debate the issues on TV. Their four debates, called the Great Debates, were watched by approximately 110 million people. On the air, Kennedy was as relaxed, calm, and self-assured as he was good-looking. He shattered Nixon's criticism that he was too young and too inexperienced for the presidency.

Nixon, on the other hand, looked tired from the vigorous campaigning and a recent knee injury. Although the first debate was a tie, Kennedy projected a better image, and his campaign took off.

On November 8, the campaigning ended and the voting began. The election was now a toss-up. Kennedy took an early lead, then faltered. Nixon led, then faltered, and so it went all night. Finally, at 9:45 the next morning, Nixon conceded defeat.

The air was cold and the streets of Washington, D.C., were covered with snow on January 20, when Kennedy took his oath of office. The theme of his stirring inaugural speech was that a "new generation" of Americans would confront the challenges of the sixties, which he called the New Frontier. He encouraged the young to act by saying, "Ask not what your country can do for you, but what you can do for your country." Intelligent, young, and vigorous, Kennedy himself symbolized the new generation seeking the New Frontier.

Kennedy also promised to defend freedom around the world. "Let every nation know, whether it wish us well or ill, that we shall pay any price, bear any burden, meet any hardship, support any friend or oppose any foe in order to assure the survival and success of liberty. This we pledge and more."

World events soon tested his words.

Top: over 70 million Americans watched the first televised debate between presidential candidates John F. Kennedy *(left)* and Richard M. Nixon *(right)*. Bottom: Vice-President Richard Nixon *(standing)* was showered with ticker tapes and confetti as he campaigned in New York in 1960. President Eisenhower *(seated)* made a rare appearance with him.

Left: on election day in 1960, John F. Kennedy gave his daughter, Caroline, a piggyback ride at their home in Hyannis Port, Massachusetts. Below: Chief Justice of the Supreme Court Earl Warren administering the presidential oath of office to John F. Kennedy at the Capitol. In his speech to the nation, the President stressed the challenges that lay ahead for all Americans, especially the young.

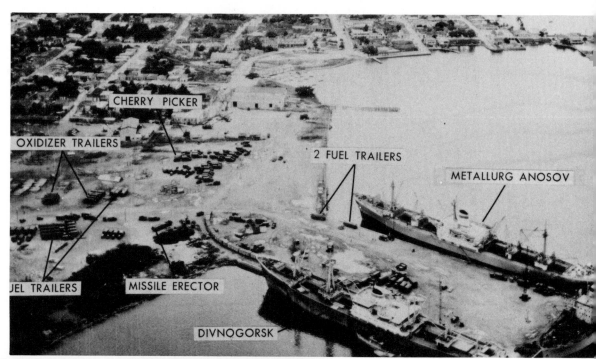

OXIDIZER TRAILERS

CHERRY PICKER

2 FUEL TRAILERS

METALLURG ANOSOV

UEL TRAILERS

MISSILE ERECTOR

DIVNOGORSK

Above: low-flying American U-2 spy planes took photographs of Cuba that revealed Russian-built missile sites and equipment. Left: a young German couple, married in West Berlin, wave across the Wall to relatives and friends in East Berlin who were not allowed to attend the ceremony.

The United States teetered on the brink of war when it backed an invasion of Cuba, an island located 90 miles (144 km) away from Florida. Fidel Castro, a rebel leader, overthrew the President of Cuba, Fulgencio Batista, in 1959. Castro then nationalized land owned by United States companies and joined forces with Russia. In 1961, non-Communist Cubans, with the support of the U.S. Central Intelligence Agency, invaded Cuba at the Bay of Pigs, in an attempt to overthrow Castro. The invasion was a fiasco and all of the invaders were killed or captured. The United States was embarrassed and forced to give Cuba $53 million worth of medical supplies and food in return for the prisoners.

A second crisis soon confronted Kennedy. Following World War II, Germany was divided and East Germany, occupied by Russia, became a Communist country. Berlin, the former capital of Germany, was located in the East; it, too, was divided. Nikita Khrushchev, the premier of Russia, pressured the United States to withdraw its troops from West Berlin. Kennedy refused and Russia responded by building a brick and barbed wire wall between East Berlin and West Berlin during the night of August 12–13, 1961. The United States protested, but eventually accepted the wall.

Crisis after crisis developed in world affairs. The United States tottered dangerously close to war when Russian-built nuclear missile sites were discovered in Cuba in 1962. The United States was outraged and Kennedy demanded the removal of the missiles. Russia refused. The President ordered United States ships to surround the island. For five days Americans waited for Russia to make a move. Children practiced air raid drills. Bomb shelters were built. Food was stockpiled. Submarines armed with nuclear weapons cruised the oceans. Then twenty-five Russian ships were spotted sailing toward Cuba. Tension mounted. Khrushchev demanded the removal of U.S. missiles from Turkey, which borders the USSR. Kennedy ignored him. The Russian ships sailed closer and closer. Near the Cuban coast, they suddenly turned around and went home. The United States won a cold war victory. Within days, the missiles were dismantled and returned to Russia.

The dramatic confrontations between the U.S. and the USSR overshadowed a war raging in a small Asian nation called Vietnam. Kennedy sent 3,200 military "advisors" to aid the non-Communist forces. No one suspected his move was a step toward our involvement in the bitter Vietnam War.

On the homefront, the goals of the New Frontier were not always met. Kennedy handled Congress poorly and his major proposals, such as funds for mass transportation systems, medical care for the aged, federal aid to schools, and civil rights legislation, were stalled.

Despite the setbacks for his programs, Kennedy was always popular. He and his wife Jacqueline were a handsome couple and they gave the White House receptions and dances an atmosphere of glamour and charm. Sophisticated, cultured, and youthful, they were for thousands the ideal American couple.

Then tragedy struck. Kennedy and his wife were riding in an open car down the crowded streets of Dallas, Texas. As the car rolled along, they smiled and waved to the crowds. Suddenly, the sound of gunshots shattered the air and Kennedy, wounded, clutched his neck. The limousine raced to the hospital and reporters raced to the telephones. The wire service of United Press International transmitted its first report at 12:39 P.M.: "FLASH. Kennedy seriously wounded. Perhaps fatally by assassin's bullet." His death was announced at 1:33 P.M. Stunned Americans wept, prayed, or stared into space in disbelief. The date was Friday, November 22, 1963.

Saturday morning, the bronzed coffin holding the dead body of Kennedy was placed in the East Room of the White House. Friends and family, political foes and allies, national and international leaders, came to pay their last respects.

The coffin was then moved to the rotunda of the Capitol in a solemn and stately procession. Tears glistened in the eyes of Mrs. Kennedy, but never fell. She presented a model of courageousness. All day and all night, mourners waited in the drizzling rain to silently file past his coffin.

Monday morning, a mass was said for Kennedy at St. Matthew's Cathedral. His body was then taken to Arlington National Cemetery for burial.

Kennedy's accused assassin, Lee Harvey Oswald, was never brought to trial. Police were bringing Oswald to a different jail when he was gunned down by tavern owner Jack Ruby. Oswald's murder left many unanswered questions about Kennedy's death. Johnson appointed the Warren Commission to investigate Kennedy's death, but their report raised as many questions as it answered.

Left: President Kennedy and his wife, Jacqueline, often gave formal balls or dinner parties that added a touch of glamour to the White House. Below left: the flag-draped coffin of John F. Kennedy was taken from the Capitol building to St. Matthew's Cathedral for the funeral mass. The riderless horse, stirrups turned in, symbolized the loss of a leader. Below right: an astonished nation watching live television saw Jack Ruby shoot Lee Harvey Oswald, the accused assassin of John F. Kennedy.

**As Jacqueline Kennedy looked on, Lyndon B. Johnson
was sworn in as President aboard *Air Force One* before
the sad flight from Dallas back to Washington, D.C.**

"The President is dead, Mr. President," said Kenneth O'Donnell, a personal aide to Kennedy. Lyndon B. Johnson was catapulted into the White House as the new President and he knew he faced difficult tasks. His goal was to make his take-over of the presidency smooth. In his first speech to Congress, Johnson said, "let us continue" Kennedy's work. Johnson personally worked to dislodge the logjam of bills backed up in Congress. Following heated debate, the civil rights bill was passed as well as a tax reduction bill.

But there was little more than a year left to Kennedy's term and Johnson soon found himself embroiled in the 1964 election. The Republicans nominated Barry Goldwater, a Senator from Arizona, as their presidential candidate. The views of Johnson and Goldwater were very different.

Johnson pledged to eliminate poverty, to restore the cities, to fight pollution, and to aid education through federal programs. As his campaign slogan, Johnson promised to create a Great Society. Most Americans were living the "good life," but there were some who were living in rat-infested tenements or shacks. In his book *The Other America,* Michael Harrington charged that there were families who were hungry in the midst of plenty. President Johnson launched a "war on poverty."

As a conservative, Goldwater was opposed to federal funding for cities and schools. He also promised to fight crime in the streets, which was viewed as an anti-civil rights position.

Goldwater advocated strong military action in Vietnam and was soon labeled "bomb crazy." The Democrats conducted a devastating smear-and-fear campaign on TV and in the press, and laughingly turned Goldwater's slogan, "In your heart, you know he's right," into "In your guts, you know he's nuts."

In contrast, Johnson was presented as the "peace" candidate. He promised to keep American troops out of the fighting in Vietnam, a promise he soon broke.

The election was really no contest. Johnson won by a landslide, capturing 61 percent of the popular vote and the electoral votes of 44 states. He immediately prodded Congress to pass the legislation he wanted in order to make his dream of a Great Society a reality. As a former Senate majority leader, Johnson knew how to win votes for his bills. The 89th Congress (1966) passed a record number of bills, which provided federal aid to schools, medical care for the aged, and grants to farmers. Congress passed the High Speed Transit Act, the Clean Air Act, the Voting Rights Act, the Child Safety Act, the Truth-in-Packaging Act, and more.

Opposite, top: top-ranking government officials, representatives from the press, and civil rights leaders watched as President Johnson signed the historic Civil Rights Act. Bottom: Arizona Senator Barry Goldwater ran against Lyndon B. Johnson in the 1964 presidential election. An ultra-conservative and supporter of the Vietnam War, Goldwater was badly defeated by Johnson. Page 14 top: President Johnson and his wife, affectionately called Lady Bird, enjoying a rare moment of quiet at their Texas ranch. Mrs. Johnson was known for her work on projects to "beautify America." Page 14 bottom: the majority of Americans enjoyed a prosperous life, but too many still lived in shacks or rat-infested tenements and survived on a meager diet. President Johnson promised to launch a war on poverty. Page 15 top: when President Johnson was photographed pulling his beagles up by their ears, the public was outraged and cartoonists from coast to coast mocked him. Page 15 bottom: the Six Day War threatened world peace. Israel crushingly defeated the Arabs and took control over the Sinai Desert, the West bank of the Jordan River, and the Golan Heights in Syria.

But despite his far-reaching reforms, Johnson was not well-liked by the public or by the press. Stories were printed alleging that he drove and drank beer at the same time, and that he picked up his Beagles by the ears. Johnson also suffered from comparisons with Kennedy, already a legend. Johnson was homely, Kennedy had been handsome; Johnson was a "country boy," Kennedy had been known as a man-about-town; Johnson spoke poorly, Kennedy had been mesmerizing.

Gradually, too, Americans became disillusioned. Buttons proclaiming "I fight poverty—I work" revealed a "backlash" against the antipoverty programs, which were costing the taxpayers millions of dollars.

Foreign affairs soon dominated Johnson's time, especially the war in Vietnam. In 1961, Johnson, then the Vice-President, told Kennedy that it was "not necessary or desirable" to send ground troops to Vietnam. Ironically, it was Johnson who built up, or escalated, the war. When Kennedy was killed, there were 16,000 "advisors" in Vietnam; in 1965, there were 190,000 troops there, and Johnson continued to escalate the war.

With American troops already in Vietnam, Johnson sent 400 Marines to the Dominican Republic on April 28, 1965. The small South American country was in a state of chaos. Rebels had overthrown the ruler Donald Reid Cabral, but no one had taken his place. Johnson feared a Communist takeover and he eventually sent 20,000 men there to oversee "free elections." Johnson was widely criticized because Americans panicked at the thought of fighting on two continents at once.

The word *war* dominated the front pages. The phone rang in the "war" room of the White House on June 5, 1967. Fearing an Arab attack, Israel struck first and attacked Egypt. Russia threatened to intervene on behalf of the Arab states and the United States rattled its sabers in its defense of Israel. On June 10, by a cease-fire agreement the Six-Day war ended, although raids and reprisals by the Israelis and the Arabs continued.

The United States escaped war in the Middle East. But its other wars were going poorly. The situation in Vietnam was grim, and the "war on poverty" was unsuccessful.

THE
LIVING ROOM
WAR

The Vietnam War was the longest and least successful war in American history. It touched every aspect of American life and brought with it frustration, protest, panic, anger, and inflation. Vietnam, a small country in Southeast Asia, was a French colony from 1867 until World War II when the Japanese took control. During the Japanese occupation, a rebel named Ho Chi Minh fought against them and gained control over the Northern section, which he named the Democratic Republic of Vietnam. When the French attempted to re-establish its rule in 1946, Ho Chi Minh fought them, too. The fighting continued for eight years until the French suffered a serious defeat and withdrew. The Geneva Accords peace treaty divided Vietnam temporarily into two zones at the 17th parallel. Free elections were scheduled for 1956 to reunite Vietnam under one leader. Ho Chi Minh ruled the North and Ngo Dinh Diem established the Republic of Vietnam in the South. But in 1956, Diem refused to allow the elections. The Viet Cong, the Communist political party founded by Ho Chi Minh, attempted to gain control over the South by a combination of goodwill and guerrilla fighting. Village leaders who refused to join the Viet Cong were kidnapped, tortured, or killed.

Top, left: helicopters streaked across the sky as they flew troops and supplies in and out of battle. Top, right: the U.S. troops fought hard, but they were unprepared for a guerilla war. Bottom: after the *USS Maddox* was attacked by the North Vietnamese in August of 1964, President Johnson retaliated with bombing raids on North Vietnam.

President Eisenhower feared the spread of Communism and he said, "The loss of Indochina will cause the fall of Southeast Asia like a set of dominoes." His famous "domino theory" led us into the Vietnam War, since he sent military "advisors" to South Vietnam to aid Diem. When Kennedy entered the White House, he followed suit. The United States military leaders predicted an easy victory.

But the South was falling apart from within. The dictatorial policies of Diem made him unpopular. The Buddhists claimed that Diem, a Catholic, discriminated against them and several Buddhist monks turned themselves into human torches in protest. Diem was finally overthrown with the tacit approval of the United States. Yet his removal brought only more chaos and unrest to the South as regime followed regime.

Meanwhile, American helicopters flew troops in and out of battle. U.S. bombers streaked across the sky at night. Yet the public was told our men were only "advisors"; they numbered 16,000 by the end of 1963.

When Johnson was propelled into the White House, he was given conflicting advice on the war. Only one thing was clear. South Vietnam was doomed without American help. Johnson stepped up military aid.

But the United States soon learned that the Viet Cong were elusive and difficult to defeat. They struck suddenly, generally during the night. Then they disappeared into the jungles and villages. There was no front line in the Vietnam War and Northern troops infiltrated the South easily. They traveled across the mountains and through the jungles of Laos into the South. Their route was called the Ho Chi Minh Trail.

A serious turning point in the war occurred on August 2, 1964. The ship, the *USS Maddox,* was attacked in the Gulf of Tonkin by North Vietnamese torpedo boats. Two days later, the *USS Maddox* and the *C. Turner Joy* were supposedly attacked by the North Vietnamese without provocation. In retaliation, Johnson ordered bombing raids on North Vietnam, a deliberate act of war by the United States.

On August 7, Congress gave Johnson the authority to take "all necessary measures to repel any armed attack against the forces of the United States or prevent aggression in Southeast Asia." This congressional action was called the Gulf of Tonkin Resolution.

Ironically, during the fall of '64, Johnson campaigned as the peace candidate against Barry Goldwater, and he repeatedly pledged that American soldiers were not going to fight in an Asian land war. His words were proven hollow.

Within months, the United States dropped bombs on the North in retaliation for Communist raids in the South. There was a pattern of more raids, more bombs, more raids, and more bombs. On February 18, 1965, the United States turned another corner in the war. Now planes bombed the Viet Cong in the South. The homes and food of the South Vietnamese peasants was destroyed in the process of defending them.

The war was not going well for the South. Johnson again escalated the American efforts. The "advisors" now numbered 30,000, and the press reported that they were engaged in battle. But the United States officially sent our first combat troops, 3,500 Marines, to Vietnam on March 8, 1965. They came ashore at Danang. The war went into high gear. Every action called for more action. Camps and bases were scourged in the jungles. Cam Ranh Bay, a natural harbor, became a bustling military port.

By the end of 1965, there were 190,000 American troops in Vietnam, 1,350 dead, and 5,300 injured.

As the war stepped up, anti-war protest stepped up. Spearheaded by students, the pros and cons of the war were debated at "teach-ins." Young men burned their draft cards in symbolic protest over the war and the size and number of anti-war marches increased. The anti-war movement was spurred by press reports coming out of Vietnam that contradicted the White House version of the war, and the press said a "credibility gap" existed in the Johnson Administration. Over 10,000 people opposing the war marched down Fifth Avenue, New York, on October 15, 1965. Despite the protest, the war went on.

At Christmastime, there was a truce. The fighting and the bombing stopped and Johnson extended the halt until January. He made offers to discuss peace with North Vietnam. His offers were ignored, and the North rapidly repaired its damaged roads and bridges. In February, Johnson gave the go-ahead for more bombing, including Hanoi, the capital of North Vietnam.

Above, left: General William Westmoreland congratulated U.S. troops on a "job well done" in Qui Nhon, South Vietnam, in 1966. Above, right: wearing the uniform of the elite military corps—the Green Berets—world-famous comedian Bob Hope entertained U.S. troops in Vietnam.

Facing page, top: the United States dropped thousands of tons of bombs on North Vietnam, but the Viet Cong continued to attack villages and cities in the South. The Viet Cong struck suddenly and then disappeared into the jungle. Facing page, bottom: U.S. soldiers in Vietnam formed a Christmas tree with the cannons of their tanks and some makeshift decorations. Facing page, right: drenched in blood pouring from his buddy's wounds, a U.S. Marine tries to comfort his friend during a battle in Hue, South Vietnam. Above: thousands of war protestors gathered in Central Park in New York City on April 15, 1967, as part of a nationwide mobilization effort against the Vietnam War.

For the first time in American history, TV cameras recorded the battles, and the Vietnam War was dubbed "the living room war." Night after night Americans saw the blood and the gore of war. They saw innocent children lying dead, wounded, or starving.

Throughout 1966 the fighting increased, the casualties increased, and the peace movement grew more militant. Students staged sit-ins at induction centers, and manufacturers of war equipment and materials were picketed. At the close of 1966, there were 425,000 American troops in Vietnam. The war was now the burden of the United States.

In February 1967, there was a Women's Strike for Peace. Many women carried signs which read: "War is unhealthy for children and other living things." On April 15 there was a nationwide Mobilization Against the War. Americans from all walks of life, of all ages, from all ethnic, racial, and religious groups, raised their voices to yell "PEACE, NOW." Some of them objected to the killing, some to the cost which was $28 billion in 1967 alone, and some to the cause. By November, only 38 percent of the American people were satisfied with Johnson's performance as President.

Yet, the war went on and the military recounted its victories. Under General William C. Westmoreland, American troops did tally up impressive gains against the enemy. But as the Americans left an area, the Viet Cong seeped back in like water through a wet rag.

Then came the crushing blow. At the start of Tet, Vietnam's holiest holiday, a seven-day truce was declared. Four days later, the Viet Cong struck with sudden, explosive attacks which went off like a string of firecrackers in 36 out of 44 provincial capitals. They struck and struck hard at 100 targets, including Danang, the largest Army base. Tan Son Nhut, a vital military airport, was shut down for days. The damage was extensive and the deaths and injuries were heavy. An unknown American officer was quoted as saying, "It became necessary to destroy the town to save it." His statement became the hallmark of the war. The Tet offensive destroyed American hopes for victory. The ragtag army of the Viet Cong, like the ragtag army of the Revolutionary War, had held a major power to a standstill. The Tet offensive was a shock, and 1968 was to bring many more surprises, all unpleasant.

AMERICA—
LOVE IT OR
LEAVE IT

As 1968 unfolded, anger, violence, and bitterness shook the United States to its roots and made their mark on the November presidential election. January brought disaster for the Pentagon. Close to the Korean coast, the *USS Pueblo* was captured by North Korean gunboats and the eighty-three-member crew was imprisoned. The United States negotiated for the return of the men. Like a sleeping giant attacked by mosquitos, the Pentagon found itself powerless to control the small countries which challenged the military force of the United States.

Seven days later, the Tet attacks by the Viet Cong further embarrassed the Pentagon. The military reports that said the United States was winning the Vietnam War were proven false. The "credibility gap" was now as wide as the Grand Canyon. Anti-war fever reached a new high.

Senator Eugene McCarthy, a longtime opponent of the war (also known as a "dove"), entered the race for the presidency. He challenged fellow Democrat Johnson in the first primary, held on March 12, in New Hampshire. McCarthy was the underdog. But over 300 student volunteers, dubbed McCarthy's Children's Crusade, canvassed the state, rang doorbells, and drummed up support for him.

Their work paid off. Johnson won by only 230 votes in a state known for its "hawks," or people in favor of the war. McCarthy's campaign was on the move. The anti-war movement won its first victory. But the unity of the doves was threatened. Robert F. Kennedy, John's brother, jumped into the race.

Johnson now made a gesture towards peace. On March 31, he announced a halt in the bombing and surprised Americans with his withdrawal from the presidential race: "I shall not seek nor will I accept the nomination of my party for another term as your President." Unbelievably, the United States was going to change leaders in the midst of a war.

April brought its own surprise. Martin Luther King, Jr., a leading civil rights leader, was assassinated in Memphis, Tennessee. Riots erupted in the black ghettos of Chicago, Detroit, and elsewhere around the country.

The street violence made "law and order" an issue in the on-going campaign. Kennedy and McCarthy were battling it out in the state primaries. Kennedy won the elections in Indiana and Nebraska. Then he lost in Oregon, giving the upcoming California primary on June 5, added importance. Though tired, Kennedy stumped up and down the state. When the votes were counted, he was the winner. But there was no victory celebration. That evening Robert F. Kennedy was gunned down. He died at 1:44 A.M. on June 6. An Arab immigrant, Sirhan Sirhan, was later arrested and convicted.

Opposite, top left: Senator Eugene McCarthy, vocal in his opposition to the war in Vietnam, lost the Democratic primary in New Hampshire to President Johnson by only 230 votes. Top right: on March 31, 1968, President Johnson made a televised address to the public to announce a bombing halt in Vietnam. He astonished viewers by concluding with his decision not to seek reelection. Bottom: Robert F. Kennedy shook hands with citizens of Sioux Falls, South Dakota, as he campaigned for the Democratic primary.

With the murder of Kennedy came an uproar for gun control and a pall of sorrow which settled over the upcoming election. Nevertheless, the political machine soon moved back into gear.

On a hot day in August, thousands of delegates to the Democratic Convention poured into the city of Chicago, the site of the meeting. They were joined by McCarthy's supporters, hippies, doves, hawks, the Mobilization Committee to End the War, and 5,000 National Guardsmen. The Yippies (members of the Youth International Party) went to Chicago planning to disrupt the Convention. The police prepared themselves for trouble, for the student "take-over" at Columbia University in New York the previous May was still etched on their minds. Protesting university policies, students had seized five buildings on campus. Files were destroyed, buildings were damaged, and students were injured in their confrontations with police. The outburst triggered demonstrations at scores of colleges and universities.

The Chicago police were instructed to clamp down on the hordes of young people demonstrating at the Convention. Aided by clubs and tear gas, the police cleared the parks in their efforts to enforce a law banning anyone from sleeping in the parks. The press called their actions a "police riot." And it was just the beginning.

Two days later, the police broke up an anti-war march taking place without a permit. The marchers and innocent bystanders were clubbed, dragged, beaten, gassed, and arrested. The police were bombarded with bottles, sticks, and stones as the mob yelled, "The whole world is watching." Indeed, it was. But the television tapes were delayed and played as the Convention nominated Hubert Humphrey. It seemed as though the United States was on the verge of chaos. And it got worse.

At dawn, the police outside the Hilton Hotel were hit with debris thrown from a window. In a blind rage, they rushed into the hotel and mistakenly attacked McCarthy's young volunteers. They beat them and terrified them until McCarthy himself brought the outburst to an end.

What a contrast to the peaceful Republican Convention in Miami where Richard M. Nixon was nominated! Nixon's only real rival for the Republican nomination was George Romney, the governor of Michigan. Romney was sabotaged by his own off-the-cuff remarks and Nixon easily wrapped up the nomination.

The violence between anti-war demonstrators and Chicago police during the 1968 Democratic National Convention in Chicago shocked Americans.

In the fall, Nixon and Humphrey squared off for the campaign and focused on two major issues: the war in Vietnam and "law and order" at home. Although Johnson had initiated peace talks in May, no treaty was within sight.

Nixon stressed the problems the United States faced. "When the strongest nation in this world can be tied down in a war in Vietnam for four years with no end in sight, when the richest nation in the world cannot manage its own economy, when a nation with the greatest tradition for respect for law and rule of law is torn apart by unprecedented lawlessness . . . then the time has come for new leadership for America!"

Humphrey stressed his commitment to help the working men and women, the disadvantaged, and the elderly. He charged Nixon with changing his political positions and told his audiences they couldn't trust Nixon.

With emotions running wild, the election was made even more tumultuous by a third candidate, segregationist George Wallace. He attacked doves, students, busing, big government, open housing, civil rights, and Communists. He played on Americans' fears and in the end captured 13 percent of the vote. Nixon defeated Humphrey with only 43 percent of the vote. His margin of victory is the slimmest on record.

Once in office, Nixon was unable to achieve an "honorable end" to the war as he promised. Negotiations dragged on, but Nixon announced his "Vietnamization" plan. It called for the gradual replacement of American troops by South Vietnamese troops. In June 1969, 25,000 American men came home from Vietnam, while over 500,000 troops remained there.

Opposite, top: Alabama Governor George Wallace made strong showings in the Democratic presidential primaries in 1968. His campaign motto "Stand Up for America" thinly disguised his anti-black position. Middle: President Johnson met with President-elect Richard Nixon to discuss world affairs. Bottom: Hubert Humphrey campaigning in Houston, Texas, only days before the election.

Facing page, top: yelling "Peace Now," thousands of demonstrators walked through the streets of San Francisco during one of many coast to coast anti-war rallies in the fall of 1969. Facing page, bottom: in Washington, D.C., a protestor holds up a sign reading "Silent Majority for Peace" in response to President Nixon's plea for the silent majority to support the war. Above: in a small village called My Lai, in South Vietnam, U.S. soldiers under the command of Lt. William Calley massacred hundreds of old men, women, and children. The Army cover-up was exposed and Lt. Calley was tried for murder.

Vietnamization continued but Americans were impatient. They wanted an immediate end to the war. On Vietnam Moratorium Day, October 15, 1969, thousands of people demonstrated and sang "Give Peace a Chance." From behind closed curtains at the White House, Nixon watched a candlelight parade of 50,000 war protestors march down Pennsylvania Avenue. M-Day sentiment swept the country like a tidal wave. But Nixon called on the "silent majority" to support him.

Despite daily photographs and TV footage of the war and its victims, the public was shocked when one of the bloodiest chapters in the history of the war was written, the My Lai Massacre. United States soldiers on a search-and-destroy mission had shot and killed over 300 old men, women, and children in a small South Vietnamese town named My Lai on March 16, 1968. The Army had tried to cover up the massacre, but *Life* magazine ran pictures of it in their December 5, 1969 issue. The commanding officer, Lieutenant William Calley, was eventually charged with murder.

My Lai was the last straw for Congress, which repealed the Gulf of Tonkin Resolution. Yet, even then, the war went on. Nixon slowly withdrew troops. But in the spring of 1970, while some troops were on their way home, other troops were on their way to Cambodia to destroy North Vietnamese supply depots. The extension of the war into Cambodia and Laos brought forth a new wave of protest in the United States.

At 441 colleges and universities across the country, students staged strikes to protest the U.S. invasion of Cambodia. The National Guard was called to Kent State University in Ohio to keep order. But the nervous Guardsmen panicked and a minor scuffle ended with the death of four students.

Yet, the war still dragged on. For two more years there was fighting and bombing as the negotiators talked. Nixon was reelected in 1972 in a landslide victory over George McGovern, whose campaign was a fiasco. Finally, on January 27, 1973, a ceasefire agreement was finally signed. The last American troops were flown home in March. The total dead numbered over 57,000. The total number wounded was over 300,000.

South Vietnam fell to the Communists in 1975.

"THE EAGLE HAS LANDED"

The New York Yankees were playing the Milwaukee Braves when the radio and television bulletins announced that the Russians had launched the world's first space satellite, *Sputnik I.* The date was October 4, 1957. Americans were startled and worried, for space power equalled military power.

The American space program came under scrutiny and was dealt a second blow when its first satellite launch attempt ended in failure. The United States finally succeeded in launching *Explorer I* on January 31, 1958. That same year, the National Aeronautics and Space Administration (NASA) went into operation. The responsibilities of NASA included everything from aviation research and development to the construction of satellites. But its most exciting goal was to send a man into space. It was called Project Mercury.

From over 100 qualified men, NASA selected seven astronauts in 1959: Alan Shepard, Jr., M. Scott Carpenter, L. Gordon Cooper, John H. Glenn, Jr., Virgil I. "Gus" Grissom, Walter M. Schirra, Jr., and Donald K. Slayton. They were given rigorous physical and mental tests and they were spun around, isolated, analyzed, and probed. While they were in training, the Russians sent the first man into space, Yuri Gagarin. On April 12, 1961, he made one orbit around the Earth in 1 hour and 48 minutes.

(35)

**Live television coverage recorded the
exciting moments of the U.S. space program.**

The first American in space was Alan Shepard. At 9:34 A.M. on May 5, 1961, his spacecraft, nicknamed Freedom 7, blasted off. Five minutes later, he fired his retro-rockets for his return to Earth. His 15-minute suborbital flight had reached a maximum height of 116.5 miles (186 km) and a maximum speed of 5,100 miles (8,160 km) per hour.

A second orbital flight was made by Gus Grissom. He landed safely in the Atlantic Ocean, but the hatch on his capsule blew off too soon and water poured into it. Grissom was rescued, but the Liberty Bell capsule sank.

President Kennedy wholeheartedly supported the space program. Now he set an ambitious goal, to go to the moon and back before 1970. "We choose to go to the moon in this decade not because it will be easy but because it will be hard," he told Americans.

The race to the moon between the United States and Russia was on. The Russians were in the lead in 1961, for they had sent their spacecraft *Vostok II* around the earth 17.5 times and Americans had yet to make an orbital flight.

Finally, on February 20, 1962, Lt. Col. John H. Glenn, Jr. was the first American to orbit the earth. On the second orbit the capsule relayed the message to ground control that the heat shield was loose. Without it, Glenn's capsule would burn up on reentry into the earth's atmosphere. But Glenn triumphantly splashed down and suffered no ill effects except skinned knuckles.

Project Mercury ended with the flight of L. Gordon Cooper. He circled the earth twenty-two times in 34 hours and 20 minutes, and he was the first astronaut to really fly the spacecraft. On the nineteenth orbit his automatic control system failed, but he took over and made a perfect landing.

The Russians were still leading in the race to the moon.

The next step in the American space program, Project Gemini, was delayed two years. Meanwhile, a second "class" of astronauts was selected.

The next outstanding moment in space literally came in space. Astronaut Ed White went outside the capsule and took a "walk" in space, while Jim McDivitt piloted the capsule of the Gemini 4 mission.

Problems plagued the Gemini 5 mission before the launch and during the flight. Astronauts L. Gordon Cooper and Charles Conrad turned off their radios and rode in silence to conserve power. For an unexplained reason, the power was very low and the astronauts were nearly ordered to return home on the first day of the mission. But power built up and the mission lasted a record eight days.

The Gemini 8 flight on March 16–17, 1966, finally accomplished a major goal of the project—docking. Neil A. Armstrong and David R. Scott tracked an Agena target in orbit and then smoothly slid the nose of their spacecraft into the docking collar of it. But then the linked vehicles went into a spin and the astronauts were forced to undock and make an emergency landing in the Pacific Ocean.

The last four Gemini flights refined the docking techniques and paved the way for the final step to the moon, Project Apollo.

The United States was catching up with the Soviet Union.

Astronauts Gus Grissom, Ed White, and Roger Chaffee were chosen to make the first Apollo flight. In their preflight checkout, there were a number of irritating problems and delays. The static on the communication system interfered with the work and Grissom yelled, "How can you expect to get us to the moon if you people can't even hook us up with a ground station?" The testing continued under an atmosphere of frustration. Then Grissom yelled, "We've got a fire in the cockpit . . . a bad fire . . . open her up . . . let's get . . . we're burning up . . ." and then there was an agonizing cry of pain. Heavy smoke covered the launch pad. After five minutes of confusion and panic, the astronauts were found dead in their seats. The first casualties of the space program occurred on a supposedly safe trial run on January 27, 1967. The exact cause of the fire is still unknown, but the investigation revealed serious errors in design. Project Apollo was delayed while every system was rechecked, modified, and rechecked again. The United States suffered a serious setback in its race to the moon.

The Apollo 9 mission, which was piloted by Jim McDivitt, Russell Schweickart, and David R. Scott, carried the first lunar module, called LM. The purpose of LM is to carry the astronauts to the surface of the moon and then return them to the command ship. Nicknamed "Spider," the LM was tested by McDivitt and Schweickart. They flew in an orbit around the moon and then tried to link up with

Above, left: the Mercury capsule, nicknamed Freedom 7, was placed on top of the rocket. Freedom 7 carried the first American astronaut, Alan Shepard, into space. Right: Alan Shepard's suborbital flight lasted only 15 minutes, but it marked the beginning of the United States–Soviet Union race to the moon. He splashed down into the ocean where he was picked up by a helicopter.

Above: Astronauts Walter Schirra *(left)* and Thomas Stafford practiced their flight maneuvers for the Gemini 6 flight, which was plagued with problems. Facing page, top: a huge aircraft, called a Pregnant Guppy, was specially designed to carry the third stage of Apollo 10's Saturn 5 rocket from the factory to Cape Kennedy in Florida. Bottom, left: a flash fire swept through the cockpit of the Apollo 1 spacecraft killing the three astronauts aboard while they were conducting a "routine" preflight checkout. Bottom, right: the lunar module, called "Spider," was photographed from the command ship on the Apollo 9 flight. Inside "Spider" were astronauts James McDivitt and Russell Schweickart, the first men to orbit the moon.

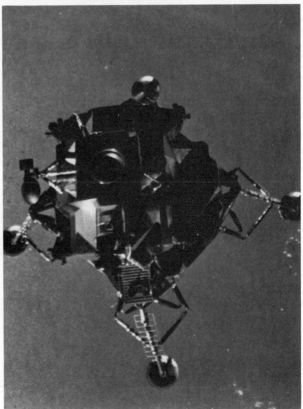

the command ship. They had difficulty lining up the two vehicles and McDivitt finally announced, ". . . I have capture." They climbed back into their command ship "Gumdrop" and aimed for home.

The command ship was nicknamed Charlie Brown and the LM was Snoopy on the Apollo 10 mission. The goal of the mission was to check out all the Apollo systems in a lunar environment, fly the LM to within 9 miles (14 km) of the moon and to scout for a landing zone on the moon. As Snoopy disappeared behind the dark side of the moon, it twisted 3½ degrees and made the undocking an uncertainty. Mission Control waited. Then as Snoopy emerged, it was flying on its own. The mission went on as scheduled. The next stop was the moon!

Cape Kennedy was filled with reporters, TV cameras, spectators, and NASA personnel. At 9:32 A.M. on July 16, 1969, *Apollo 11* was launched for a trip to the moon. Neil A. Armstrong was in command, accompanied by Lt. Col. Edwin "Buzz" Aldrin, Jr. and Lt. Col. Michael Collins. Traveling 24,300 miles (38,500 km) per hour, they reached the moon in three days and entered a lunar orbit. Armstrong said, "This view is worth the price of the trip." Armstrong and Aldrin climbed into the LM, named *Eagle,* and went into orbit. The *Eagle* moved closer and closer to the moon. All was silent. Then came the words, "Tranquility Base here. The *Eagle* has landed." The time was 4:17 (EST) on the 20th of July when the first men landed on the moon.

Outside, a TV camera was set down to record man's first step on the moon. Armstrong stepped off the LM ladder and said, "That's one small step for man, a giant leap for mankind."

As Armstrong and Aldrin collected rock samples and dirt, Collins orbited in the command module. For 2 hours, 13 minutes, and 12 seconds, Armstrong and Aldrin walked and worked on the moon. The *Eagle* and the command ship *Columbia* docked smoothly and turned for home. Splashdown occurred safely on July 24.

The United States had won the space race.

Top: astronaut Edwin "Buzz" Aldrin, Jr., descends the steps of the lunar module ladder as he prepares to walk on the moon. Bottom: following their trip to the moon, astronauts Neil Armstrong, Michael Collins, and Edwin E. Aldrin, Jr., were quarantined aboard the *USS Hornet*. President Nixon came to congratulate them on their successful mission.

Both the war in Vietnam and the space race pumped billions of dollars into industry and spurred new technological developments designed to make life more comfortable, more luxurious, and more efficient.

The scientific and technical discoveries made by NASA were turned to practical use in medicine, in the home, and in industry. The need to keep the spaceships as light and compact as possible led to the development of microelectronics. Thousands of circuits are compressed in tiny, electronic "chips," which are not much larger, and a lot thinner, than a matchhead. The "chips" led to small hand-held calculators and minicomputers.

More complex and smaller in size, computers revolutionized business. On the light side, they created a fad for "computer dating." Computers matched up couples on the basis of questionnaires.

"Live via satellite" sums up how the communications industry benefited from the space program. Echo, the first satellite visible with the naked eye, was sent up by NASA in 1960. Its aluminum mylar skin reflected communications signals back to Earth.

Telstar was the first communications satellite that was owned by a company, AT&T, and not by the government. Telstar transmitted live TV coverage of European events.

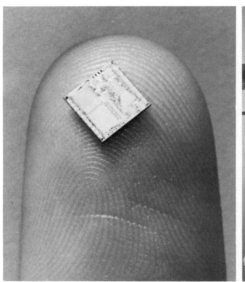

Top, left: microelectronic "chips" contain thousands of circuits despite their small size. The chips make hand-held calculators and small computers possible. Top, right: computers revolutionized business, but they also replaced names with numbers and often the young rebelled against an impersonal society. Bottom, left: large, luxurious cars like this 1965 Chevrolet were a symbol of prosperity. However, not only did they require a great deal of gasoline, they also emitted significant amounts of carbon monoxide. Bottom, right: Telstar, owned by AT&T, was the first non-government communications satellite. It transmitted live TV coverage of European events.

Top, left: in 1967, as a result of widespread concern over the environment, the Reynolds Aluminum Company pioneered recycling of aluminum cans in Los Angeles. Top, right: oil spills from tankers and offshore wells polluted the water and the coastal land. Birds, like these waterfowl, became covered with oil and died. The increasing need for oil conflicted with environmental concerns. Bottom, left: thousands of shad were victims of pollution in the Anacostia River in Washington, D.C. Bottom, right: caught in a plastic 6-pack holder, this ring-billed gull starved to death.

The scores of space spin-offs include the development of electronic pacemakers, which stimulate weak heart muscles, new alloys for artificial limbs, nonflammable materials and paints, freeze-dried foods, digital clocks, aluminum foil, Teflon, and plastic railroad cars.

The growth of industry created the "good life" for most Americans, but the price was high—polluted air, soil, and water. Industrial wastes poured into streams and lakes and killed fish and plants. *The Cleveland Press* ran one newspaper article entitled "Lake Erie Is Dying—Does Anybody Care?" to demonstrate the extent of pollution, even in major waterways. Throughout the United States, nearly 12 million fish died in 1965 alone, as a result of pollution. Health officials found that even fish caught in the middle of the ocean were contaminated with dangerous chemicals, such as mercury.

Pesticides, such as DDT, seeped into the soil and water and disastrously upset the food chain. The best-selling book *Silent Spring,* by Rachel Carson, warned the country about the dangers of disturbing the balance of nature.

Like the water and soil, the air was polluted. The cars of the sixties poured out significant amounts of carbon monoxide, a gas which causes headaches, dizziness, and sometimes death. In addition, pollutants were produced by almost every manufacturing process and by the burning of heavy fuel oil, coal, garbage, and leaves.

As the decade wore on, the public and the government pressured industrial plants to clean up their wastes. In 1965, President Johnson declared, "There is no excuse for a river flowing red with blood from slaughterhouses. There is no excuse for paper mills pouring tons of sulfuric acid into the lakes and streams. There is no excuse for chemical companies and refineries using our major rivers as pipelines for toxic wastes. There is no excuse for communities to use the people's rivers as a dump for raw sewage." Mrs. Johnson, nicknamed Lady Bird, led a campaign to beautify America. Congress responded to the environmental problems by passing the Federal Water Quality Act, the Endangered Species Act, the Wilderness Act, and the Clean Air Act.

By the late sixties, a back-to-earth movement was in full swing. Recycling centers were set up for newspapers and bottles. Vacant lots littered with garbage were cleaned up and turned into "people's parks." Organic foods, grown without the use of pesticides, were sold in health stores, and rural farm communes dotted the landscape. In short, Americans rediscovered the beauty of nature.

BLACK IS BEAUTIFUL

Joseph MacNeill, a black college student, walked into a Woolworth's department store in Greensboro, North Carolina, on February 1, 1960, and ordered a ham sandwich and coffee. The waitress refused to serve him. He was angry, but he was not surprised, because blacks were often treated as second-class citizens. Blacks were the last-hired and the first-fired from work. Blacks were forced to drink from fountains marked "colored."

The next day, Joseph and three of his friends returned to the lunch counter and quietly sat down. They were refused service, but they stayed in their seats. Finally, they were dragged out and beaten, while reporters and TV news reporters watched. This sit-in set off a chain reaction.

Within months, sit-ins were staged in restaurants and movie theaters in cities throughout the South. CORE (Congress of Racial Equality) and the NAACP (National Association for the Advancement of Colored People), two civil rights organizations, trained students in techniques of nonviolent protest. The demonstrators were pushed and shoved by angry whites, rubbed with ketchup and mustard, jailed, and often beaten. Hurt by the bad publicity, nationwide chains like Woolworth's finally agreed to serve black customers. The integration of lunch counters marked the first of many civil rights victories in the sixties.

Left: in the early sixties blacks and whites picketed airline offices to protest laws that discriminated against blacks, often called Jim Crow laws. Below: sit-ins at lunch counters finally forced large chain stores to integrate. The first sit-in occurred in Greensboro, North Carolina, in 1960.

Top, left: George Wallace, Governor of Alabama from 1963 to 1966, was a segregationist who tried to block integration of the schools in his state. Religious leaders picketed against his position, labeling separate facilities for blacks and whites "immoral." Top, right: James Meredith resting during his march across Mississippi. The march was an attempt to prove blacks were safe from mobs in the South. Ironically, he proved just the opposite, for he was shot while marching, but not killed.

The sit-in movement gave birth to the Student Nonviolent Co-ordinating Committee (SNCC), sometimes called Snick. SNCC led thousands of students in sit-ins, wade-ins (organized to integrate pools and beaches), and pray-ins. During the fifties, the blacks scored important victories for equal rights in the courts; now they marched to insure their rights.

In 1955, the Supreme Court ruled that racial segregation on buses, trains, and planes was illegal. Five years later, the Court said that segregated stations and waiting rooms are also illegal, but the laws were never enforced. CORE organized Freedom Rides to pressure the federal government into enforcing the laws.

On May 4, 1961, two buses of blacks and whites left Washington, D.C., for New Orleans. When they reached South Carolina, a black entered a "white" waiting room at a bus station. The freedom riders were then mobbed and beaten by angry whites who had gathered to wait for the buses. In Alabama, the bus was burned by the Ku Klux Klan, and the riders were again beaten. Robert F. Kennedy, the attorney general of the United States, dispatched federal marshals to control the mobs. Throughout the summer there were many Freedom Rides, and slowly the segregation of public places disappeared as police officials complied with the Supreme Court ruling.

School desegregation was a tougher battle. The Supreme Court had ordered the integration of schools "with all deliberate speed," in 1954. Eight years later, there were still no integrated schools in Alabama, Mississippi, or South Carolina. Many schools had only token integration.

James H. Meredith, a black veteran, sought admission to the University of Mississippi. Governor Ross Barnett blocked the door to the registration office and white students mobbed and taunted Meredith. Kennedy sent federal marshals to the university to restore order and to escort Meredith to his classes. This was a landmark case because the federal government took control over a state institution. Blacks demanded the busing of black students to white schools and vice versa to achieve racial balance. The courts agreed, but the issue sparked bitter debates, clashes, and boycotts by both blacks and whites.

Black leaders organized a massive Freedom March in Washington, D.C., on August 28, 1963, to prod Congress into passing a civil rights bill. Over 200,000 blacks and whites went to the capital by car, bus, train, plane, or foot. Linked arm and arm, they sang the freedom song "We Shall Overcome." The keynote speaker was Martin Luther King, Jr., a Baptist minister and well-known black leader. Speaking at the foot of the Lincoln Memorial, he told the audience: "I have a dream that one day this nation will rise up and live out the true meaning of its creed: 'We hold these truths to be self-evident that all men are created equal.' "

The Civil Rights Act was finally passed in 1964 and Lyndon B. Johnson signed it. The new law prohibited the segregation of public accommodations and job discrimination on the basis of sex, religion, or race. Under the new law, the federal government was allowed to cut off funds to schools which failed to integrate.

But the hardest battle for blacks was still not won. To gain political and economic power, blacks needed the right to vote. They were often denied voting rights, especially in the South. Local laws, known as "Jim Crow laws," required poll taxes or literacy tests. Blacks were sometimes asked ridiculous questions, such as, "How many feathers are on a chicken?" Unable to answer, the blacks were then "failed." Organizations such as SNCC, CORE, the NAACP and the SCLC (Southern Christian Leadership Conference), sent workers to the South to encourage blacks to register to vote. The Mississippi Project Volunteers were harassed, but they continued their work.

Congress finally passed the Voting Rights Act in 1965. The new law gave federal officials the authority to check registration and voting procedures in order to protect the rights of blacks.

Facing page, top: in 1963, black leaders organized a Freedom March to prod Congress into passing a civil rights bill. Leading the march is the Rev. Martin Luther King, Jr. Left: Martin Luther King, Jr., walks black children to a former all-white school in Grenada, Mississippi. Right: President Johnson signs the historic Voting Rights Act while congressional and civil rights leaders watch.

Yet, blacks were losing patience with the Democrats and Republicans. Stokely Carmichael, a young SNCC worker, founded a new party, which adopted a panther as its symbol. Carmichael was the prime minister of the Black Panthers from 1967–69, and he made the term "black power" popular, and emphasized the need for black self-determination. The Panthers organized community stores and schools.

This new militancy often frightened whites, who were already distressed by the racial riots which had erupted. A riot in Watts, a black neighborhood in Los Angeles, California, shocked the nation. The houses in Watts were one-story pastel-colored buildings, not decaying tenements. But blacks in Watts, particularly the young, faced the problems of blacks everywhere: low wages, unemployment, and inferior schools. Their frustration with their living conditions was expressed in looting and burning the houses and stores. "Burn, baby, burn" was the battle cry of the rioting blacks. National Guardsmen, armed with bayonets and machine guns, were called in to patrol the streets. Thousands were arrested, thirty-three were killed, and millions of dollars worth of goods and buildings were stolen, broken, or burned.

Riots occurred in approximately 150 cities, including, Detroit, New York, Philadelphia, Chicago, and Newark, N.J., between 1964 and 1969. Often the Black Panthers attempted to "cool" the cities. The worst riots took place the day that Martin Luther King, Jr., was assassinated, April 4, 1968. Ex-convict James Earl Ray was convicted of the murder, but questions still remain about his guilt or innocence.

In a word, "Negro" became "black" in the sixties. Blacks took pride in their heritage, their customs, and their looks. Natural or Afro hairstyles were the rage. Blacks discovered that "black is beautiful."

Facing page, top: blacks rioted in Newark, New Jersey, for five days in July 1967. Buildings were burned, stores were looted and damaged, and many people were injured. Bottom: Stokely Carmichael, who founded a new party, the Black Panthers, preached a policy of black power.

(55)

John F. Kennedy first spoke for, and to, the young. In his inaugural address he said "the torch has been passed to a new generation of Americans," who will change the country. And they did.

Students were in the forefront of the protest movements of the decade. They spoke out for civil rights, against the war, and for the environment. They were crusaders.

But change comes slowly and a sizeable number of young people became disillusioned. They dropped out of society and created a sort of counterculture.

The new creed was "Tune in, turn on, drop out." It was first espoused by Timothy Leary, a Harvard professor who was fired for supplying LSD to his students. LSD is an hallucinogenic or psychedelic drug that causes visual and auditory illusions. LSD was legal in California until 1966, and it was to the Haight-Ashbury section of San Francisco that the dropouts or "hippies" flocked.

The counterculture, or hippie world, was dominated by drugs, especially LSD (acid) and marijuana (pot). The hippies scorned conventional fashions and wore outrageous clothes and long hair. Music, especially hard rock, was closely tied to the hippie culture, and often both the performers and the fans were high on drugs at concerts.

The first "be-in" was held in San Francisco on Saturday, January 14, 1967. It was a celebration of life, a day of drugs, poetry,

(56)

Above, left: a love-in in Newark, New Jersey.
Above, right: a long-haired "flower child"
rebels by burning his parking summons.

Above, left: Jesus was "rediscovered," especially by the young who rejected materialism and drugs. Above, top right: body painting was popular in the sixties. Above, bottom right: a funeral for the Death of Hip was held in its birthplace, the Haight-Ashbury section of San Francisco in October 1967. Ironically, the hippie movement was still growing in most other cities across the country.

rock music, and love. It marked a new beginning for Haight-Ashbury. The publicity surrounding the "be-in" enticed more and more kids to San Francisco, including "plastic hippies" who returned to home and school in the fall.

Slowly, Haight-Ashbury began to change. The streets and "crash pads" became overcrowded. The acid was now illegal, often adulterated, and the number of "bad trips" multiplied. Motorcycle gangs and drug pushers moved into the area. The leaders of Haight-Ashbury gave a funeral for the Death of Hip, and the first wave of hippies left. Some traveled from crash pad to crash pad in Volkswagen vans decorated with psychedelic art. Many moved to communes in the country.

Ironically, as the hippie movement was dying in its birthplace, it was making its mark on society. The hippies paved the way for the "do-your-own-thing mood" that was becoming as American as apple pie. Uninhibited attitudes toward sex and drugs gave rise to the label "Swinging Sixties." The hippies affected everything from fashion to politics. They popularized jeans, tie-dyed shirts and blouses, love beads, and paisley prints. They spurred the publication of underground newspapers. They led the way for the eighteen-year-old vote.

Yet, the hippies were a minority. While they dropped acid, young soldiers in Vietnam dropped bombs. While hippies were reading the novels of Ken Kesey, McCarthy's supporters were reading campaign literature. But whatever they did, the "new generation" changed society.

They rebelled against an impersonal society. Everyone had a cause in the sixties, and buttons said it all. Often the buttons they wore read "Do not spindle, fold or mutilate—I am a student." Young people sought an identity and an inner peace through drugs, religion, meditation, and analysis.

The quest for spirituality also led to an interest in Eastern religions and philosophies. The Hare Krishnas' goal is "pure eternal bliss" which can be obtained by dedication to Krishna, Supreme Lord of the Universe. The number of practitioners of Eastern religions is actually small, but thousands studied their philosophies.

The search for answers about life also led to a renewed interest in astrology. "What's your sign" was a common greeting, and the astrological symbols were plastered on everything from key rings to gold pendants.

The loud rebellious rock 'n roll of the fifties faded and the early sixties were dominated by the more "mellow" sounds of groups like the Beach Boys.

But in Great Britain rock was exploding into a new sound that was brought to the United States by The Beatles: John Lennon, Paul McCartney, George Harrison, and Ringo Starr. America was never the same after The Beatles stepped off the plane for their first American appearance. The Beatles made rock a cultural, as well as a musical, event.

Posters reading "The Beatles Are Coming" were plastered on billboards all over the United States. When they stepped off the plane at Kennedy Airport, they were greeted by thousands of screaming fans. About three fourths of all TV viewers watched them on "The Ed Sullivan Show," on February 9, 1964. Two months later, five of their songs moved up to the five top places on the charts: "I Want to Hold Your Hand," "She Loves You," "Love Me Do," "A Hard Day's Night," and "Please Please Me." Written by Lennon and McCartney, all the songs were simple, melodic, and rhythmically strong.

The same year, The Beatles made their screen debut in *A Hard Day's Night.* The movie was a parody of themselves and their second movie *Help!* was a colorful fantasy.

The Beatles performance on "The Ed Sullivan Show" of February 9, 1964, attracted almost 75 percent of all TV viewers. Though criticized for their long hair, it was short compared to future hairstyles.

**Top: Ravi Shankar, the world's leading sitar player, was a major
influence in The Beatles' later music. Bottom: hard-hitting rock
and roll, as well as the wild stage performances of Mick Jagger,
always assured The Rolling Stones of sellout audiences.**

The Beatles' next album, "Rubber Soul" (1965), reflected a musical turning point in their career. The songs "In My Life," and "Michele" were more complex lyrically and musically than their earlier work.

In 1966, The Beatles toured the United States and drew enormous crowds for all their concerts. Lennon said, "We're more popular than Jesus Christ now and I don't know which will go first: rock 'n roll or Christianity."

The release of the album "Sgt. Pepper's Lonely Hearts Club Band" (1968) was a major event. Musically, the songs were a blend of synthesized rock, and styles that ranged from Oriental to classical to jazz. The lyrics were subjected to an astonishing array of interpretations. "Lucy in the Sky with Diamonds" was said to be a hymn to LSD. The Beatles insisted their songs were not related to drugs, but the fans ignored them.

The album cover also sparked heated discussions. On it was a montage of famous people surrounding The Beatles, dressed in colorful band uniforms. A grave surrounded by marijuana plants supposedly meant The Beatles were giving up drugs and turning to meditation and yoga. This theory was reenforced when they left for India to study Transcendental Meditation under Maharishi Mahesh Yogi.

When they returned, The Beatles formed their own record company, the Apple Co., and recorded the songs for the movie *Yellow Submarine,* a cartoon fantasy. Their next album was a culmination of their growth as musicians. The cover was totally white and the album is popularly called "The White Album." Their individual styles were clearly heard on it and there were rumors that The Beatles were planning to split. But they stayed together until 1970.

In one decade, they had left behind an indelible mark on American culture.

The Beatles were the leaders of a "British invasion" on the American rock world. In the mid-sixties, The Rolling Stones recorded their first big American hit, "I Can't Get No Satisfaction," an openly sexual song.

The Rolling Stones' concerts were always sellouts. A large part of the attraction was the wild stage performances of lead singer

Mick Jagger. In 1969, they made a number of performances to push their newest album "Gimme Shelter." The Stones climaxed their tour with a free concert at the Altamont Raceway near San Francisco. Their goodwill gesture ended bitterly. Unable to get police protection, The Stones hired a motorcycle gang to keep order and to guard the stage. Instead, the Hell's Angels started a confrontation which ended in the death of a fan.

Rock 'n roll groups didn't totally dominate the music scene, however. Greenwich Village in New York was the center for a revival of folk music in the sixties. It was there that Bob Dylan was discovered. He wrote and sang songs about the hot issues of the day, civil rights, the Vietnam War, and nuclear bombs. Sung in a raspy voice, his album "The Times They are A-Changin'" (1964) captured the mood of the early sixties. The song "Blowin' in the Wind" was adopted as an anthem of the civil rights movement and the re-recording by the trio Peter, Paul, and Mary was a number one hit. Dylan's songs "Maggie's Farm" and "Subterranean Homesick Blues," accompanied by electric guitars, were the first examples of folk rock.

Simon and Garfunkel's first big hit came in 1966 with the album "Parsley, Sage, Rosemary, and Thyme," which contained the songs "The Dangling Conversation," "Scarborough Fair," and the "The 59th Street Bridge Song (Feelin' Groovy)." They wrote the songs for the sound track of the movie *The Graduate,* and "Mrs. Robinson" was a smash single hit. Their best-selling album "Bridge Over Troubled Waters" (1970) summed up the world situation.

All types of music flourished during the sixties. Soul music was an extension of rhythm and blues songs. Aretha Franklin became known as "Lady Soul."

Diana Ross and the Supremes had five number one hits in a row from 1965–66, including, "Where Did Our Love Go?" They recorded for Motown, an independent company with the motto, "It's what's in the grooves that counts."

"Acid rock" was born in the mid-sixties in San Francisco, and swept the nation in the late sixties. During performances of rock bands like the Jefferson Airplane, whirling and pulsating images were projected on the walls. The continuously changing colors and

Top, left: folksinger Bob Dylan, discovered in Greenwich Village, New York, recorded the first folk-rock songs. Top, right: Simon and Garfunkel's first big hit was the 1966 album "Parsley, Sage, Rosemary, and Thyme." Bottom: The Temptations featured the falsetto voice of Eddie Kendricks *(center)*. Their first big hit was "The Way You Do the Things You Do" in 1964.

Facing page, top: Janis Joplin *(seated)* embodied the free spirit of the counterculture. Bottom, left: Jim Morrison and The Doors gave intense and sometimes shrieking performances on stage. Bottom, right: the performances of Jimi Hendrix were wild and ear-splitting. He played a right-handed guitar upside down. Above: the top performers of the decade sang at the three-day music festival in Woodstock, New York, in 1969. Over 400,000 fans showed up, and traffic was blocked for miles.

shapes, plus the pounding beat of the music, was supposedly like a trip on LSD. The acid rock bands were said to be frequently high when they performed.

The Monterey Pop Festival (June 16–18, 1967) brought the Jefferson Airplane to the attention of RCA. Their first album "Jefferson Airplane Takes Off" was a major hit although there was no hit single on it. Two hits, "Somebody to Love" and "White Rabbit," were on their second album "Surrealistic Pillow." Their songs were generally about love or drugs, and lead guitarist Jorma Kaukonen was known for his stunning improvisations. Hit followed hit until the group fell apart in the early seventies. Surprisingly, the group was reformed in 1974 as the Jefferson Starship.

The Grateful Dead was one of the few acid rock groups to survive during the seventies. Their albums cannot capture the excitement of their live performances, but their album "Live/Dead" comes close.

The career of Janis Joplin took off after her pulsating performance at the Monterey Pop Festival. Dressed in skintight pants and outrageous clothes, she gave her performances her all. Her hoarse voice made "Cheap Thrills" a best-seller. Janis Joplin embodied the free spirit of the counterculture and personified the dropouts who drank and took drugs. She was found dead of a drug overdose on October 3, 1970.

Like Janis Joplin, Jimi Hendrix died of an overdose of drugs. His performances were wild and earsplitting. Left-handed Hendrix played a right-handed guitar upside down and he made it produce astonishing sounds.

Music was an integral part of the culture of the sixties and a concert in Woodstock, New York, was a culmination of the entire philosophy of the counterculture. About 60,000 fans were expected for the 3-day concert, but over 400,000 showed up. The fans listened to the top performers of the decade: Joan Baez, Janis Joplin, the Grateful Dead, the Jefferson Airplane, the Who, Crosby, Stills, and Nash, all types of music from folk to acid.

Despite rain, inadequate food and water, and overcrowding, there was no violence. And when it all ended the fans cleaned up the mess.

THE VAST WASTELAND

Television was labeled the "vast wasteland" in 1961 by Newton N. Minow, the chairperson of the Federal Communications Commission. The label stuck because all three networks aired the same programs: westerns, silly comedies, game shows, and police shows. The critics often said the commercials were better than the shows.

The screwball comedies of the sixties were very popular. The wackiest sit-com was "The Beverly Hillbillies." Basically, the hillbillies outwitted the city slickers. Buddy Ebsen starred as Jed Clampett, but it was Irene Ryan, as Granny, who usually stole the show.

Family sit-coms presented a new TV fad—the single parent. The fathers and mothers were always widowed. Divorced parents were not shown until the seventies. Fred MacMurray starred in "My Three Sons." Diahann Carroll starred in "Julia," as a widowed nurse working for an ill-tempered doctor.

Spies spied on every channel. In "The Man from U.N.C.L.E." Robert Vaughn starred as agent Napoleon Solo and David McCallum as agent Illya Kuryakin. They fought against the sinister organization THRUSH.

Top: agents Napoleon Solo (Robert Vaughn, *center*) and Illya Kuryakin
(David McCallum) on "The Man from U.N.C.L.E." often found themselves
entangled with beautiful women. Bottom, left: television critics during
the sixties often claimed the commercials were better than the shows,
especially this award-winning Alka Seltzer commercial. A catchy tune
played as the camera focused on all kinds of stomachs. Bottom, right:
Vince Edwards starred as the rude but competent doctor on "Ben Casey."

Top, left: "Get Smart," starring Don Adams as agent Maxwell Smart, spoofed the spy programs. Top, right: "The Smothers Brothers Comedy Hour" was a madcap variety show in which they mocked everything and anything. Pat Paulsen *(center)*, a dry-witted humorist, ran a mock campaign for the presidency in 1968. Bottom: "Bonanza" was a horse opera that galloped off with top ratings. Dan Blocker, Lorne Greene, Pernell Roberts, and Michael Landon *(left to right)* starred as the Cartwright family.

"Mission: Impossible" was built around complicated spy missions. Highly technical devices and brilliant disguises helped the Force make their entrances and escapes.

"I Spy" broke new ground in 1965 because it portrayed a black man working closely with a white man as U.S. agents.

Don Adams starred in the spoof "Get Smart." As agent Maxwell Smart, he bumbled all his assignments for C.O.N.T.R.O.L., and his weapons never worked, but he succeeded in his battles against K.A.O.S.

Medical programs reached epidemic proportions during the sixties. Two enormously popular doctors began their TV practice in 1961, "Dr. Kildare" and "Ben Casey."

Westerns reached their peak in the fifties and slowly faded away during the sixties, except for two adult westerns: "Gunsmoke" and "Bonanza." "Gunsmoke" (1955–75) was not a traditional western. Marshal Dillon (James Arness) occasionally made mistakes. Miss Kitty (Amanda Blake) provided romantic interest.

"Bonanza" galloped off with top ratings for most of the sixties. The plots concerned the problems and adventures of the Cartwrights who owned the huge Ponderosa ranch.

A time of unrest, the sixties were ripe for jokes about politics and life-styles. "Rowan and Martin's Laugh-In" was a madcap comedy hour in which everything and anything was mocked.

"The Smothers Brothers Comedy Hour," like "Laugh-in," was a tremendous hit. Religious jokes, comments about Vietnam, and protest songs, made Tommy and Dick Smothers controversial. They also annoyed the CBS censors and the show was canceled.

Carol Burnett came to the screen in 1967 and her show was highly rated for eleven years. She developed several characters for her comedy routines including her most famous—a charwoman.

The most dramatic moments on TV occurred during the coverage of actual events, such as the moon walk.

LAVISH! STAR-STUDDED!!

To compete with TV, the movies of the sixties were often expensive and lavish productions, especially musicals, such as *West Side Story* or *My Fair Lady*. The biggest musical hit was *The Sound of Music,* which starred Julie Andrews.

The large-screen epics were popular because they were packed with stars and scenery. *Lawrence of Arabia* was shot on location in the Middle East and it starred (among others) Alec Guinness, Anthony Quinn, and Peter O'Toole. *Tom Jones* (1963) was a bawdy film about a young man's sexual adventures in the eighteenth century. Julie Christie, Alec Guinness, and Omar Sharif starred in *Dr. Zhivago,* the story of the Russian Revolution and a man and woman caught up in it. *Cleopatra* starred Elizabeth Taylor and Richard Burton whose affair made the headlines. Despite the publicity, *Cleopatra* was not a box office success.

The cold war of the fifties and early sixties was reflected in spy movies. The greatest spy of them all was James Bond, alias 007. A fictional character created by Ian Fleming, Bond made his movie debut in *Dr. No.* Bond, played by Sean Connery, returned to the screen in *From Russia With Love, Goldfinger, Thunderball, You Only Live Twice,* and *Diamonds are Forever.* The plots called for exaggerated villains and bizarre murder weapons. Other spy movies include *The Ipcress File, The Deadly Affair,* and *The Spy Who Came in from the Cold.*

Antiwar feelings were reflected in *Dr. Strangelove or How I Learned to Stop Worrying and Love the Bomb* and *M*A*S*H. Dr. Strangelove* was a story about an insane U.S. general who launches a nuclear attack against Russia. *M*A*S*H* was a bitter comedy, set in a mobile army hospital during the Korean War.

2001: A Space Odyssey is the story of a man's exploration of the universe as he seeks the origin of an artifact found on the moon.

The civil rights movement paved the way for movies such as *To Kill a Mockingbird, In the Heat of the Night, Raisin in the Sun, Nothing But a Man,* and *Guess Who's Coming to Dinner,* which starred the popular black actor Sidney Poitier.

The youth movies were dismal failures except for *The Graduate* and *Easy Rider.* Dustin Hoffman was wildly praised for his role as Benjamin, a college graduate. He returns to the home of his wealthy parents where he tries to find himself while having an affair with his mother's friend. In *Easy Rider* two hippie motorcyclists take off on a jaunt to New Orleans. Dennis Hopper, Peter Fonda, and Jack Nicholson starred. Made for $400,000, *Easy Rider* grossed over $4,000,000 and established a trend toward low-budget "personal" movies.

THE AGE OF AQUARIUS

Broadway suffered a decline in the sixties because production costs skyrocketed and sent the price of tickets up. The biggest successes were musicals: *A Funny Thing Happened on the Way to the Forum,* a farce set in ancient Rome about a slave who promised to secure Philia for his master in return for his freedom. *Man of La Mancha* made the song "The Impossible Dream" a hit. Robert Morse starred in a satire on rags-to-riches stories, *How to Succeed in Business Without Really Trying. Funny Girl* made Barbra Streisand a star. She portrayed the life story of Ziegfeld showgirl Fanny Brice. *Hello Dolly,* the story of a matchmaker in New York in the 1880's, shattered box office records with its succession of leading ladies: Carol Channing, Ginger Rogers, Ethel Merman, and Pearl Bailey.

Neil Simon is a master of light comedies. Two of his shows, *The Odd Couple* and *Barefoot in the Park,* were simultaneous hits on Broadway.

The notable dramas of the decade include, *The Caretaker,* by Harold Pinter, *Who's Afraid of Virginia Woolf?* by Edward Albee, and *The Night of the Iguana,* by Tennessee Williams. Nicol Williamson gave an excellent performance in Shakespeare's classic *Hamlet.*

The most provocative and daring plays were produced off-Broadway. Unlike Broadway, off-Broadway and regional theaters flourished in the sixties. *Hair,* the most controversial musical of the decade opened on off-Broadway in 1967. The plot focuses on a young man torn between burning his draft card or going to war. *Hair* was brought to Broadway the following year and new songs about pollution, sex, drugs, military service, and religion were added, plus a nude scene. Condemned as "vulgar" and "dirty" by some critics, *Hair* was hailed by other critics. The unconventional dialogue and action made the rock musical a symbol of the new rebellious generation. *Hair's* song "The Age of Aquarius" was a sensational hit.

CATCH-22

The book publishing industry thrived and the number of new titles published between 1960 and 1970 doubled. Young people, especially

**Top: Sean Connery starred in the early James Bond films, including
Goldfinger. Bottom, left: *Hair* was a controversial rock musical, later
made into a movie. Bottom, right: Barbra Streisand was a top recording
star, Broadway performer, and movie actress in the sixties. Her performance in the musical *Funny Girl* propelled her into the limelight.**

college students, made the works of Hermann Hesse, Kurt Vonnegut, J. R. R. Tolkien, and Gunther Grass popular. Hesse's novels *Steppenwolf* and *Siddharta* deal with the search for life's meaning. Vonnegut wrote a number of books dealing with the problems of the twentieth century, including *Cat's Cradle* and *Slaughterhouse Five*. *Lord of the Rings,* by Tolkien, is a trilogy of fantasy stories. German novelist Grass satirized the Nazi era in *Dog Years*.

Joseph Heller wrote *Catch-22*, which is a classic example of bitter, or black, comedy. The novel is about an American Air Force unit in Italy during World War II. The hero keeps trying to get out of flying more missions. But the doctor can't ground him even though he says he's crazy.

"You mean there's a catch?"

"Sure there's a catch," answered the doctor. "Catch-22. Anyone who wants to get out of combat duty isn't really crazy."

Norman Mailer was the leading author of the "new journalism." He told about events such as the antiwar march on the Pentagon in personal terms in *The Armies of the Night*.

Books by black authors, such as *The Fire Next Time,* by James Baldwin, and *The Autobiography of Malcolm X,* were widely read as a result of the civil rights movement.

EYE-POPPING

The boldest works of art in the sixties were pop art and op art. The subjects of pop art were everyday objects, such as Coke bottles. Andy Warhol was a leader of the pop art movement. His silk screen prints of actress Marilyn Monroe and of a Campbell soup can are world famous.

Claes Oldenburg specialized in creating very large versions of ordinary things like hamburgers. Roy Lichtenstein is notable for his large paintings of comic strip frames.

Pop art merged art and reality. Sometimes pop art was reality. Jasper Johns made sculptures from light bulbs and wire and coffee cans!

Op art (short for optical) are pictures which appear to move. The designs of Victor Vasarely, the "father" of op art, are based on mathematical principles.

"I am the greatest. I am the prettiest," Muhammad Ali told everyone everywhere. And he certainly was the most colorful and most controversial athlete of the decade. Boxing champ Ali wrote and recited doggerel verse predicting the outcome of his fights and called his opponents names in and out of the ring.

Muhammad Ali won the title of heavyweight champion of the world on February 25, 1964, when he defeated Sonny Liston, the favorite. Liston put his entire 220 pounds behind his punches and he was again favored to win a rematch in 1965. Ali flattened him in the first round.

Following his defeat of Liston, Muhammad Ali joined the religious sect the Black Muslims. That's when he gave up his "slave" name Cassius Clay, and took the name Muhammad Ali. Muhammad means "worthy of all praises" and Ali means "the most high."

In 1963, the Louisville draft board for the armed services classified Ali as 1-Y (not suitable). But in 1966, he was reclassified 1-A and drafted. He asked for an exemption from service as a conscientious objector to the war. His request was denied and the army ordered him to take his service oath on April 28, 1967. Ali refused and was arrested for draft resistance. The World Boxing Association and the New York State Athletic Commission immediately stripped him of his title.

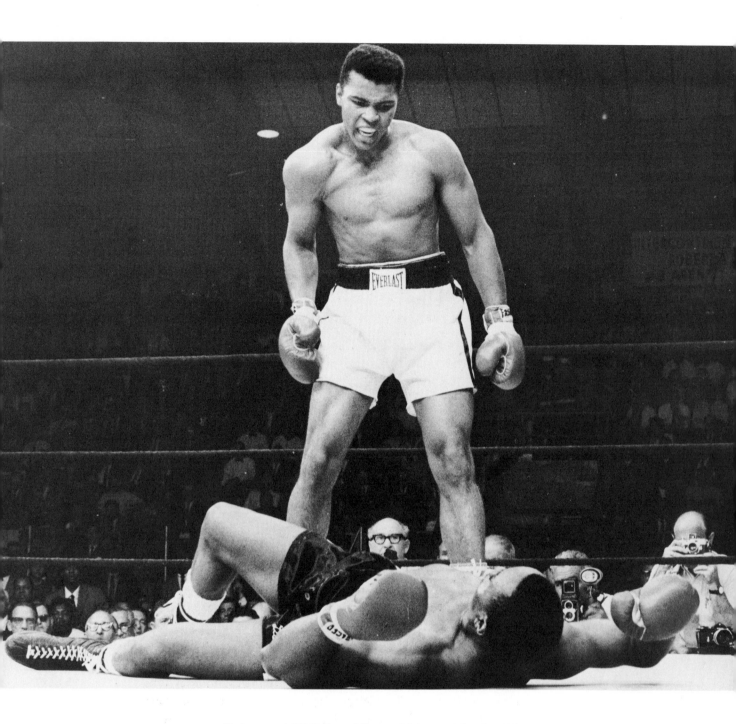

**Muhammad Ali flattened Sonny Liston to win the 1965
rematch for the heavyweight championship of the world.**

Following a highly publicized trial, Ali was found guilty of draft evasion. He was fined $10,000 and received a sentence of five years in jail. He appealed the verdict and he remained free, but he was unable to fight.

When Ali was stripped of his title, the crown was disputed. On February 16, 1970, Joe Frazier was named champion. Meanwhile, Ali attempted to regain the right to box.

Frazier and Ali finally fought in March 1971 at Madison Square Garden, Ali was knocked down in the fifteenth round for the first time in his career. He staggered to his feet and went the last four rounds, but Frazier was named the winner in a hotly contested decision by the judges. Ali, however, won a more important victory. The Supreme Court, in an 8–0 decision, ruled that he was entitled to refuse the draft on religious grounds. Ali became a free man and a folk hero.

Frazier lost his title to George Foreman in 1974. Foreman, in turn, lost the crown when he was later knocked down by Ali.

UP FROM THE CELLAR

The New York Yankees and the Los Angeles Dodgers were the powerhouse teams on the diamond. The Yankees boasted two outstanding players: Mickey Mantle and Roger Maris. In 1961, Maris hit 61 homeruns and Mantle hit 54. Switch-hitter Mantle holds the record for homers during a World Series (18).

In the 1962 season, Dodger Maury Wills stole a record 104 bases. But the Dodgers lost the National League pennant to the Giants, who were then defeated by the Yankees in the Series.

The Dodgers defeated the Yankees in four straight games to win the Series in 1963. They won again in 1965 when Sandy Koufax pitched a no-hitter. He became the first man in history to pitch four no-hitters, and he did it in four years.

The team that captured the hearts of the fans was the New York Mets. The Mets joined the National League in 1962 and finished in last place for five years and next-to-last for two years. Amazingly, the Mets climbed out of the cellar and won the National League pennant in 1969. They went on to play the Baltimore Orioles in the Series. The Orioles were sluggers and won the first game. But the

Above: Dodgers' pitcher Sandy Koufax pitched four no-hitters in four years. Facing page, top: Maury Wills steals his record-breaking 104th base during the 1962 season. Bottom, left: in 1961, New York Yankee Roger Maris hit 61 home runs in a single season. Bottom, right: Mickey Mantle was a powerful batter for the New York Yankees in the 1960s.

Mets came back to win the second, third, fourth, and fifth games as their fans roared with delight.

WINNING—THE ONLY THING

The name which dominated football in the sixties was Vince Lombardi. He was the coach of the Green Bay Packers and he brought them from last place in the National Football League to first. Lombardi is famous for saying "Winning isn't everything. It's the only thing." The Packers won five world championships in his nine years as coach. Packer Paul Hornung was the best all-around offensive player in the NFL and he held the NFL record with 176 points in a single season.

One of the most colorful football players was Joe Namath. He played for the New York Jets, a member of the American Football League. Namath led the Jets and they captured the AFL title in 1968. In a dramatic game they surprised the fans by defeating the NFL champs, the Baltimore Colts, in a 16–7 victory. It was the first Super Bowl championship for the AFL.

THE STILT

The Boston Celtics had won the National Basketball Association title every year except 1967. Bill Russell was the outstanding player and he led the League in rebounds for four years. From 1967 to 1969, Russell was both a player and the coach, the first black coach in NBA history.

Facing page, left: Joe Namath of the New York Jets was one of the most colorful football players of the decade, both on the field and off. Top right: coach Vince Lombardi led the Green Bay Packers to five world championships in nine years. Bottom right: seven-foot-one-inch Wilt Chamberlain of San Francisco flies toward the basket to score two points in a game against the New York Knicks in 1964.

1968 Olympic medalists in the 200-meter dash, Tommie Smith *(center)* **and John Carlos raise their fists in a black power salute while the band played "The Star-Spangled Banner."**

Bill Russell's rival on the courts was Wilt "The Stilt" Chamberlain. In his first year with the Philadelphia Warriors (1959–60) he broke the one-season pro scoring record. He averaged 37.6 points per game. The next season he made 3,000 baskets in a season, a new record. He continued to break records. He broke three records in a single game against the New York Knicks: he made 36 field shots and 28 out of 32 foul shots to give him a record 100+ points in one game.

GRAND SLAM

Rod Laver dominated tennis, winning all the major tennis championship matches. In 1969, he became the first tennis player in history to win two grandslams, all the major tournaments in one year.

In women's tennis, Billie Jean King dominated the courts. She won all the major tennis matches in singles and doubles. As an outspoken advocate of equality for women, she fought for more recognition of female athletes.

THE OLYMPICS

The 1960 Olympics, held in Rome, saw new records set in ten out of thirteen track events, and eight of nine field events. Rafer Johnson, a student at the University of California, performed spectacularly and won the decathlon. Muhammad Ali, who made front page history in the sixties, won a gold medal for light heavyweight boxing.

It was Wilma Rudolph, however, who gave the spectators their biggest thrill. She overcame polio at the age of eight, and at the age of twenty she won three gold medals for the 100-meter dash, the 200-meter dash, and the 400-meter relay quartet.

The 1964 Summer Olympics held in Japan are most notable because for the first time the games were broadcast live via satellite.

The name associated with the Winter Olympics of 1968 is Jean-Claude Killy. He captured the gold medals in skiing for the slalom, the giant slalom, and the downhill, an astounding feat which made him an instant star. An American, Peggy Fleming, won a gold medal for women's ice skating. She, too, is a celebrity now.

The Summer Olympics of 1968 were a success for the United States. The American team captured 50 percent of the medals for track and field events for men. In swimming, the United States won eleven of seventeen events for men, and twelve of sixteen for women.

But the Olympics also caused the U.S. an embarrassing moment. Black runners Tommie Smith and John Carlos came in first and third, respectively, in the 200-meter dash. During the awards ceremony they raised their fists in a black power salute as "The Star Spangled Banner" was played. They were sent home at once.

THE END OF THE SWINGING SIXTIES

The decade of the sixties was a manic time. Spirits soared and then lunged as unforgettable events unfolded. Quiet moments were rare, for it was an age of causes. It seemed as though there were daily demonstrations for peace in Vietnam, and civil rights, and against nuclear power, police brutality, and busing. Questions were raised about the schools, the churches, the government, the military, and the corporations. The decade teemed with charismatic leaders, triumphs, and defeats. The trademark of the sixties was extremism in everything from politics to art to fashion. They were incredible years.

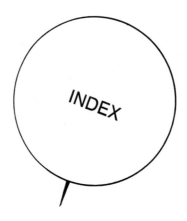

INDEX